Festivals *of the* World

SWITZERLAND

Gareth Stevens Publishing
MILWAUKEE

Written by
SUSAN MCKAY

Edited by
GERALDINE MESENAS

Designed by
LYNN CHIN

Picture research by
SUSAN JANE MANUEL

First published in North America in 1999 by
Gareth Stevens Publishing
1555 North RiverCenter Drive, Suite 201
Milwaukee, Wisconsin 53212 USA

For a free color catalog describing Gareth
Stevens' list of high-quality books and multimedia
programs, call
1-800-542-2595 (USA)
or 1-800-461-9120 (Canada).
Gareth Stevens Publishing's Fax: (414) 225-0377.
See our catalog, too, on the World Wide Web:
http://gsinc.com

© TIMES EDITIONS PTE LTD 1999
Originated and designed by
Times Books International
an imprint of Times Editions Pte Ltd
Times Centre, 1 New Industrial Road
Singapore 536196
Printed in Singapore

Library of Congress Cataloging-in-Publication Data:
McKay, Susan.
Switzerland / by Susan McKay.
p. cm.—(Festivals of the world)
Includes bibliographical references and index.
Summary: Describes how the culture of
Switzerland is reflected in its many festivals,
including the Children's Festival, the William Tell
Festival, and Silvesterklause.
ISBN 0-8368-2027-4 (lib. bdg.)
1. Festivals—Switzerland—Juvenile literature.
2. Cookery, Swiss—Juvenile literature.
3. Switzerland—Social life and customs—
Juvenile literature. [1. Festivals—Switzerland.
2. Holidays—Switzerland. 3. Switzerland—
Social life and customs.] I. Title. II. Series.
GT4864.A2M39   1999
394.26'09494—dc21   98-30451

1 2 3 4 5 6 7 8 9 03 02 01 00 99

CONTENTS

28 July 99 Book Farm 14.95

It's Festival Time . . .

Many people think of Switzerland as a quiet, picturesque country. No doubt it is one of the most beautiful countries in the world, but during Switzerland's celebrations, it is anything but quiet! Clanging cowbells, yodeling from mountaintops, and brass bands playing *Guggenmusig* [GOO-gen-MOO-zig] are the order of the day at festival time. So come and join in the burning of the *Boogg* [BOOG], wrestle Swiss-style, and make fondue! It's festival time in Switzerland . . .

WHERE'S SWITZERLAND?

Switzerland lies in the heart of Europe. It borders France to the west, Germany to the north, Italy to the south, and Austria and Liechtenstein to the east. It is a small country that can be crossed by car in only one day. Despite its small size,

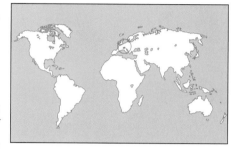

there is no shortage of natural wonders in Switzerland, with its many lakes, mountains, and valleys. There are also modern cities in Switzerland, such as Zurich, Geneva, and Basel. Bern is the capital of the country.

A Swiss girl with a basket of bread.

Who are the Swiss?

The Swiss are as varied as their countryside. Many years ago, warriors came to Switzerland from Germany, France, and Italy to conquer the land. These people eventually settled in the country and mixed with the Romans and Celts already living there. Years later, immigrants came to Switzerland from all across Europe. The Swiss today have four national languages—French, German, Italian, and Romansh (a language originating from the ancient Romans.) These languages reflect the country's **diverse** ethnic background.

SWITZERLAND

GERMANY

FRANCE

AUSTRIA

LIECHTENSTEIN

ITALY

• Schaffhausen
• Basel
Winterthur •
• Aarau
• Zurich
• St. Gallen
• Appenzell
Lake Zurich
• Solothurn
Luzern •
• Neuchâtel
BERN
Lake Lucerne
• Altdorf
• Fribourg
• Davos
• Interlaken
Jura Mountains
S
• Gruyères
• St. Moritz
• Gstaad
Lake Geneva
• Montreux
P
• Geneva
A
L
• Lugano
• Matterhorn
Lake Maggiore

N

A beautiful lakeside scene in the
Swiss countryside with a splendid
view of the Alps.

WHEN'S THE CELEBRATION?

WINTER

- ✪ **SAINT NICHOLAS DAY**—Children receive gifts, and villagers wear huge headdresses in processions to honor Saint Nicholas.
- ✪ **ESCALADE**—Commemorates the day in 1602 when the Duke of Savoy tried unsuccessfully to conquer the city of Geneva.
- ✪ **CHRISTMAS EVE AND CHRISTMAS**
- ✪ **ENGADINE**—Unmarried girls and boys wear traditional Swiss costumes and travel from village to village in decorated sleds.
- ✪ **SILVESTERKLAUSE**
- ✪ **VOGEL GRYFF**—Participants dress up in costumes of three mythical figures—the wild man of the woods, a griffin (a mythical lion with an eagle's head), and a lion.
- ✪ **FASNACHT**

The Fasnacht will be starting soon. Join us as we march with the others in this colorful parade on page 12!

SPRING

- ✪ **SECHSELAUTEN**
- ✪ **EASTER**
- ✪ **ASCENSION DAY**—Priests ride on horseback to bless the crops.
- ✪ **CORPUS CHRISTI**—The streets of towns and villages are carpeted with flowers to commemorate the crucifixion of Christ.
- ✪ **MAY DAY**—A girl and boy are named May Queen and King and lead a procession through their village.

SUMMER

- ✪ **CALLING OF THE COWS**
- ✪ **ALBANIFEST**—The town of Winterthur is transformed into a fairground, with thrilling rides, food stalls, music, and dancing.
- ✪ **CHILDREN'S FESTIVAL**—Nearly 8,000 children participate in a parade featuring bright costumes, flowers, and grilled sausages.
- ✪ **MONTREUX JAZZ FESTIVAL**
- ✪ **FESTIVAL OF THE GUARDIAN ANGEL**—After a morning church service, participants travel on foot to a cave where they eat and dance for the rest of the day.
- ✪ **SWISS NATIONAL DAY**—Commemorates the formation of the Swiss confederation in 1291.
- ✪ **WILLIAM TELL FESTIVAL**

Wow! This headdress is very heavy. See other elaborate headdresses worn for New Year's celebrations on pages 8-11!

AUTUMN

- ✪ **BACHFISCHET**—Villagers in Aarau catch fish before the annual cleaning of the stream. Children carry branches and flowers in a parade, after which there is a shared meal of fish cooked over a fire.
- ✪ **KING OF THE MARKSMEN**—A traditional rifle match held in Zurich.
- ✪ **VINTAGE FESTIVAL**
- ✪ **CHILBI**—Alpine festivals celebrated with yodeling, wrestling, dancing, and music.
- ✪ **SAINT MARTIN'S DAY**—In most towns across Switzerland, people make turnip lanterns to represent the light and faith Saint Martin brought into the lives of the people he met.

7

SILVESTERKLAUSE

I n the tiny town of Urnasch in the Appenzell region, the folk festival year begins on January 13th with *Silvesterklause* [sil-VEST-er-klauz]. This ancient festival dates far back to the days when the Swiss used a different calendar. Silvesterklause is basically the Swiss New Year.

How is it that the New Year falls on January 13th in Switzerland? Keep reading to find out!

This picture shows Pope Gregory XIII sending missionaries to England.

Old New Year

The calendar many of us use today is called the Gregorian calendar. It was named after Pope Gregory XIII. The old calendar, called the Julian calendar, was slightly inaccurate, losing almost one day every century. So, in 1582, Pope Gregory revised the Julian calendar to more closely correspond to the movement of Earth around the sun. Silvesterklause celebrates the Old New Year, or the beginning of the year according to the ancient Julian calendar.

A boy with a giant cowbell around his neck. On Silvesterklause, almost everyone wears a cowbell. It's no wonder, then, that this is such a noisy event!

How is it celebrated?

At the crack of dawn on New Year's Eve (January 12th), costumed men called Silvesterklause ("Spirits of the New Year") arrive at the center of the village. The men dress in elaborate costumes made from natural materials, such as twigs, moss, and branches. Many of them wear huge headdresses with beautifully carved scenes from everyday life in the Swiss countryside. These headdresses are sometimes so heavy they hurt the wearer. The costumes are decorated with bells, either thirteen round bells or two giant cowbells strapped to the front and back. When the Silvesterklause reach the village square, they dance and sing to announce their arrival. Then, they walk in groups from house to house singing wordless yodels to wish the villagers a happy New Year. After good wishes have been exchanged, the Silvesterklause clang their bells to ward off evil and move on to the next house. They do this until midnight, when they stop to celebrate the New Year with the rest of the villagers.

The Silvesterklause go from house to house greeting the villagers with yodels, a traditional Swiss greeting.

Yodeling

Yodeling is a kind of singing almost always associated with Switzerland. Throughout the country, many yodeling competitions are held. This form of singing is believed to have originated with the Alpine peoples of Switzerland and Austria, but you can also hear yodeling in the mountain areas of China and North and South America. Some people think it may have started as an imitation of the alpenhorn, a traditional Swiss instrument played at festivals and other celebrations. The alpenhorn is a long horn made entirely from pine and can be over 33 feet (10 meters) long. To see what the alpenhorn looks like, turn to page 21.

Above: On Silvesterklause, don't be shocked to see a tree walking toward you. It's only a man dressed in a costume made from twigs, leaves, and other natural materials.

Below: A yodeling group celebrates its victory in a yodeling competition.

Kafi Menzberg

Why is it called Silvesterklause?

December 31st is the feast day of Saint Silvester, who was pope from A.D. 314–335. According to legend, Constantine, the Roman emperor at the time, fell deathly ill. He begged his **pagan** priests to cure him, but they could not. Finally, he called on the pope. Silvester cured Constantine by baptizing and converting him to Christianity. After this, Constantine built many churches and gave Christians freedom of worship. This event marked the beginning of the Christian Roman Empire.

Look at the beautiful costumes and headdresses on these villagers in Urnasch! The town holds one of the most spectacular Silvesterklause celebrations in the country.

Think about this

During the rule of Constantine, Christians were forbidden to practice their religion. Many Christians fled to the hills to escape from Roman soldiers. Constantine's conversion to Christianity was a very important historical event. It meant that all Christians could worship God openly and freely.

11

FASNACHT

At exactly four o'clock in the morning on the Monday before Ash Wednesday, all the lights in the city of Basel go out. This is the *Morgenstreich* [MOR-gun-STRIKE], when costumed participants pour into the streets with their lanterns. When the people start beating their drums and playing their pipes, everyone knows that Basel's *Fasnacht* [FASS-nukt] celebrations have begun!

Above: A colorful Clique with their equally colorful lantern.

Opposite: Piccolo players in front of the City Hall in Basel.

Join the Clique

The people of Basel form groups called Cliques for the Fasnacht celebration. Each Clique creates a lantern and costumes based on a **theme**. The lanterns are big and colorful creations, covered with rhymes. If you can get close enough, you can even read the rhymes—but only if you understand Swiss German! New lanterns are made every year and are illuminated from the inside for the Morgenstreich, when the Cliques display their lanterns and costumes in a huge procession through the streets of Basel.

Left: Children love the Fasnacht, when they can dress up as their favorite animals!

12

Guggenmusig

The Tuesday before Ash Wednesday belongs to children and Guggenmusig, a funny version of a popular song played by a brass band. It is a special day for the children. They march in groups through the streets in colorful masks and costumes. Some dress up as *Waggis* [wah-GEES] who chase people and throw confetti on them. Don't worry if you are caught—you may still receive a flower for your trouble!

The *Guggenmusiker* [GOO-gen-MOO-zik-er] and band leader with his colorful band behind.

Honoring the lanterns

Fasnacht in Basel lasts exactly three days and ends at four o'clock Thursday morning. As a final event, the participants honor the lanterns by playing a march and gathering around the lanterns. When the conductor signals the musicians to stop playing, the lights are put out, and the three beautiful days are over.

Beautiful multi-colored lanterns on display during the Fasnacht festivities in Basel.

Not like other Carnivals

Fasnacht in Basel is unlike any other Carnival around the world. There are parades but no dancing in the streets, and there is sometimes a touch of anger in the air. Although Fasnacht is the time for a final celebration before Lent, traditionally it has also been a time of political rebellion. Some people use Fasnacht as a time to protest against the government. Others simply relax and enjoy the festivities.

These are the mischievous Waggis that chase people and throw confetti on them. Don't let them catch you!

15

SECHSELAUTEN

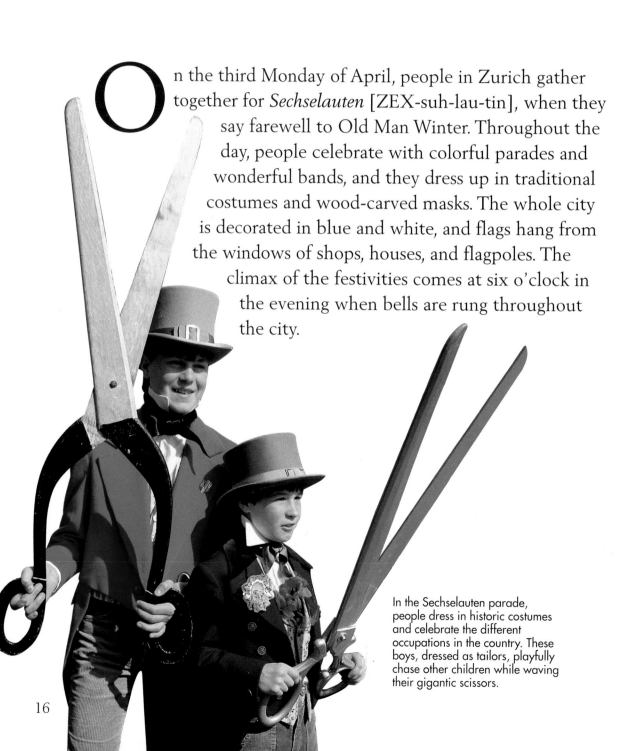

On the third Monday of April, people in Zurich gather together for *Sechselauten* [ZEX-suh-lau-tin], when they say farewell to Old Man Winter. Throughout the day, people celebrate with colorful parades and wonderful bands, and they dress up in traditional costumes and wood-carved masks. The whole city is decorated in blue and white, and flags hang from the windows of shops, houses, and flagpoles. The climax of the festivities comes at six o'clock in the evening when bells are rung throughout the city.

In the Sechselauten parade, people dress in historic costumes and celebrate the different occupations in the country. These boys, dressed as tailors, playfully chase other children while waving their gigantic scissors.

16

The parade

On the Sunday before Sechselauten, a parade is held to honor children, but the main attraction starts at 12 noon the next day, when members of the 25 **guilds** of Zurich dress in historic

Above: Young children in colorful historic outfits rule the day in the children's parade.

costumes and parade through the city center. Shops and offices close, and people flood the streets to get a glimpse of the floats and costumes. People dressed as tailors playfully chase children while waving oversized scissors. Those dressed as bakers hand out pastries, and gifts are thrown to the crowds.

The rain interrupts the parade sometimes—it is, after all, still winter. But the fun is not spoiled for these girls waiting to start their parade down the street.

17

The burning of the Boogg

At about five o'clock in the evening, the Sechselauten parade heads south along the river until it reaches the tip of Lake Zurich. Here, in a large, empty clearing, is a huge woodpile, stacked nearly 33 feet (10 m) high. Teetering on top of the woodpile is Boogg, a snowman made of cotton wool and stuffed with fireworks. He is an **effigy** of winter.

Above: The Boogg is paraded through the streets by guildsmen in medieval costumes.

At exactly six o'clock in the evening, bells begin to chime, signaling the start of the grand event—the burning of the Boogg. A hush falls over the crowd as groups of men on horseback, wearing **medieval** armor and carrying swords, circle the snowman. The woodpile is doused with gasoline and set on fire.

Flames creep up the woodpile, and, soon, Boogg's whole body is in flames. At the final moment, Boogg explodes with pops, bangs, and plenty of color.

The Boogg is burned by the side of Lake Zurich.

The calculation

According to tradition, the guildsmen must monitor the exact time it takes for Boogg to explode. Then, a series of complicated calculations are made to determine how many days are left until spring. The sooner the snowman burns, the faster spring will come.

What is Sechselauten?

The word *sechselauten* means "six o'clock ringing." The ringing of city bells is an ancient tradition that originated in the fourteenth century to signal the end of the summer working day. The guilds used to take part in the governing of the city, but, today, they just participate in the fun.

These men dressed in medieval costumes are heading toward Lake Zurich, where the Boogg will be burned. On this day, even the horses are dressed up!

CALLING OF THE COWS

Just as the Swiss hold a festival to celebrate the end of winter, they also hold one to celebrate the beginning of summer. Each year, near the end of May and sometimes through June, the sound of cowbells can be heard throughout the mountains of Switzerland. It sounds like a concert, but it is actually the Calling of the Cows, an ancient tradition that marks the start of summer.

This boy is wearing the traditional costume of the alpine farmer, while his cow is decorated with flowers and bells in celebration of the start of summer.

Leaving the valley

At the end of spring, tens of thousands of cows leave the valley pastures and climb high into the mountains to the alpine meadows. This is part of the natural **migration** of the animals to their summer feeding grounds. Each region of Switzerland celebrates this event in a different way, but all of them begin with a procession. The men who herd the cows dress up in traditional costumes, and the cows are decorated with flowers and bells.

Alpenhorns are wooden horns that measure over 33 feet (10 m) in length! Alpenhorn blowing takes a lot of skill, and many competitions are held during the year to see who blows the alpenhorn best!

Music and dancing

Once the procession is over and the crowds have reached the highlands, the music and dancing begin. Men dressed in wool trousers with patterned straps and suspenders blow on alpenhorns, while others participate in flag-tossing competitions. The women, dressed in silk aprons and long-sleeved jackets, get the traditional dancing underway.

Swiss wrestling

Young and old alike use the festival as a way to demonstrate their strength and skill. Swiss-style wrestling, for example, is a traditional sport that is usually performed during the festival and on other special occasions. Two competitors wear cotton or leather shorts over their pants. The aim of Swiss wrestling is to lift the other person off the ground. The winner is the one who succeeds.

Above: Traditional Swiss wrestling is a popular festival activity that draws a large crowd.

Swiss wrestling takes place in a sand pit. Two wrestlers try to lift each other off the ground by grasping each other's **torso**.

Cow fights

In some areas of Switzerland, cow fights are very popular. The more **aggressive** cows are chosen, and two such cows are brought face to face for a match. There is, however, no need to worry about the animals being treated cruelly because cows normally fight with each other to establish which is the stronger cow. In fact, this is the way **hierarchies** are established in many animal groups, such as lions, elephants, and wolves. In these matches, the cows are rarely harmed because they do not injure each other. The winner becomes queen of the herd and wears an enormous cowbell as a prize.

Think about this
A similar festival takes place when the cows are brought back down to the winter pastures. Life in the countryside is often dictated by the changing of seasons. Festivals are held to mark the move from one season to the next.

Around the middle of May, cow fights are held in many areas of the Swiss countryside. You cannot always get your cow to fight though—cows only fight when they feel like it!

WILLIAM TELL FESTIVAL

Every year in July, the Swiss honor one of their greatest heroes—William Tell. This festival takes place in the small town of Interlaken in central Switzerland. Interlaken is situated on a lake, and the lake becomes the setting for a play called *Wilhelm Tell* ("Wilhelm" is the German way of saying "William.") Many people make special trips to Interlaken to watch the play. So, who was William Tell, and why is a play about him so popular? Read on and find out!

The drama

In 1804, a German playwright named Friedrich von Schiller wrote a play called *Wilhelm Tell* based on a popular Swiss legend. He used the area around Lake Lucerne (check the map on page 5) as the setting. The play was so moving that it became a worldwide success. Today, the spirit of William Tell is revived every year at Interlaken, when 80 actors take to the stage to put on Schiller's play.

This painting shows the legendary William Tell about to shoot an arrow through the apple on his son's head. Notice the cruel Gessler's hat on a pole in the middle of the picture.

The legend of William Tell

Many Swiss cannot decide if William Tell was a real person or just a myth, but all agree he is one of Switzerland's greatest heroes. About 700 years ago, Switzerland was ruled by Emperor Rudolf of Austria. Rudolf sent a governor named Gessler to rule in the region where William Tell lived. Gessler was a terrible man who thought he was very important. He took away people's land and money.

One day, Gessler put his hat on a pole in the town center and made all the townspeople bow to it to show their respect. When it was William's turn to bow, he refused. Gessler became very angry and wanted to punish William. He forced William to shoot an apple from off his son's head. Fortunately, William was an excellent marksman, and the arrow split the apple in two without hurting the boy. William saved his second arrow for Gessler, whom he shot through the heart. It was soon after this incident that the Swiss gained their independence from Austria. William Tell became a hero to the Swiss people and a symbol of freedom.

25

THINGS FOR YOU TO DO

The Swiss have many traditional costumes that vary from region to region. These costumes are the pride of the people and are worn on the many festive occasions the Swiss celebrate throughout the year. Swiss costumes are bright and colorful, and many display the traditional Swiss craft of embroidery.

Costumes of Switzerland

Herdsmen of the Appenzell region have one of the most colorful and distinctive costumes. They wear short, sleeveless red jackets with little flowers embroidered on the lapels and suspenders that carry pictures of the herds they tend. An Appenzell herdsman also wears a silver earring in his right ear and a hat decorated with flowers and ribbons. In Gruyères, herdsmen wear short blue jackets with short gathered sleeves and edelweiss embroidered on the lapels. Natives of the Bern region wear small black caps and matching short black jackets with red trim and embroidered flowers on the lapels.

Make an Appenzell herdsman's hat

An Appenzell herdsman's costume is bright and colorful, but it is not complete without its special hat! To make an Appenzell herdsman's hat, you need glue, scissors, a black hat, several stalks of small, colorful flowers, and two ribbons—one red and one green. Glue the two ribbons on the back of the hat. Then, cut the stems off the flowers and stick them onto the hat in whatever color combination you like—use your imagination! When you're done, put on your brightest clothes and your Swiss hat, and you can be an Appenzell herdsman for a day!

Things to look for in your library

Cooking the Swiss Way. Helga Hughes (Lerner Publications, 1995).

Heidi. Johanna Spyri and Eileen Hall (translator) (Puffin Classics, 1995).

Mandie and the Singing Chalet. Lois Gladys Leppard (Bethany House, 1991).

Swiss Holiday. Elizabeth Yates and Gloria Repp (Bob Jones University Press, 1996).

Switzerland. Goldberg-Werrenrath Productions (Journal Films, 1985).

Switzerland: The Summit of Europe. Discovering Our Heritage (series). Margaret Schrepfer (Dillon Press, 1989).

William Tell. Leonard Everett Fisher (Farrer, Strauss & Giroux, 1996).

MAKE A COWBELL

Traditionally, cowbells were attached to cows as they were led up the Alps in summer. Today, decorating cowbells has become an art, and the Swiss often hang beautifully decorated cowbells outside their homes. During Silvesterklause, cowbells are even hung around people's necks and rung for good luck. Follow the simple steps below and make your very own cowbell!

You will need:
1. A large paper cup
2. Silver or gold foil
3. Glue
4. A small bell
5. Scissors
6. Painted macaroni
7. String

1 Cover the large paper cup with silver or gold foil. Glue the ends inside the cup.

2 With the scissors, poke a small hole in the bottom of the cup. Thread string through the hole and tie a knot. Make sure the string is long enough to go around your head.

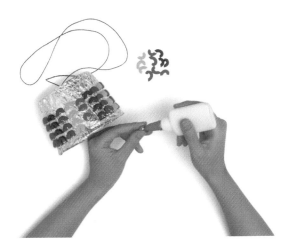

3 Attach the small bell to the string on the inside of the cup.

4 Glue macaroni on the outside of the cup. You can use as many pieces of macaroni as you want, in as many colors as you like! When you are finished, you have your very own cowbell! Wear it around your neck and ring it for good luck!

MAKE SWISS FONDUE

E mmentaler and Gruyère are well-known Swiss cheeses and are the main ingredients in the famous Swiss dish, fondue, where chunks of white bread are dipped into melted cheese. According to tradition, anyone who lets bread fall into the cheese has to buy drinks for the evening!

You will need:
1. A pot
2. 2 two-pronged forks
3. 1¼ cups (300 ml) apple juice
4. Measuring spoons
5. Chunks of white bread
6. 1 tablespoon butter
7. 1 teaspoon cornstarch
8. ½ teaspoon nutmeg
9. 1 clove crushed garlic
10. An oven mitt
11. 9 oz. (250 g) grated Gruyère cheese
12. 9 oz. (250 g) grated Emmentaler cheese
13. A wooden spoon

1 and 2

3

4

5

6

7

8 and 9

10

11

12

13

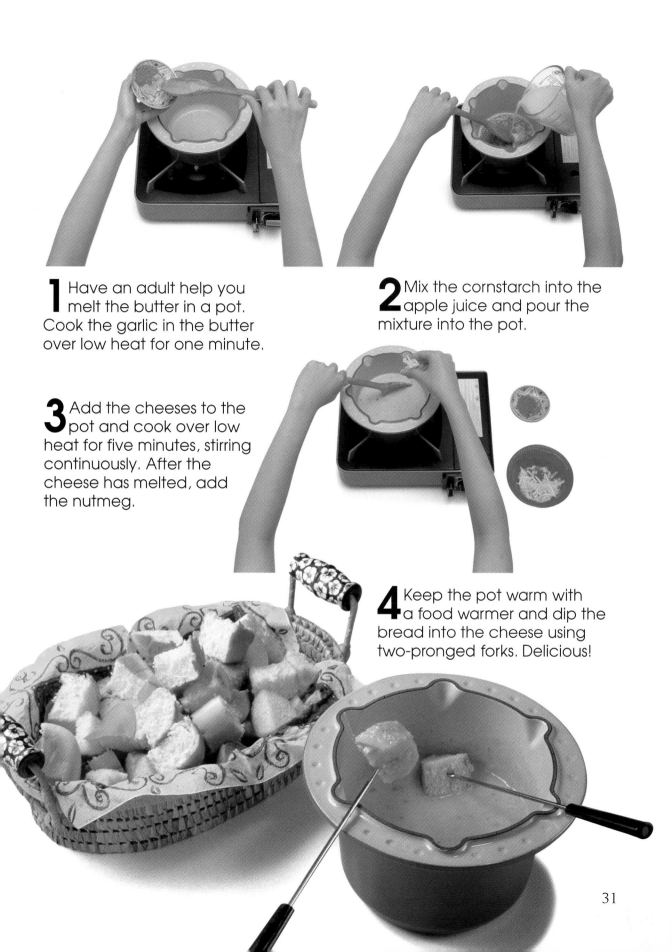

1 Have an adult help you melt the butter in a pot. Cook the garlic in the butter over low heat for one minute.

2 Mix the cornstarch into the apple juice and pour the mixture into the pot.

3 Add the cheeses to the pot and cook over low heat for five minutes, stirring continuously. After the cheese has melted, add the nutmeg.

4 Keep the pot warm with a food warmer and dip the bread into the cheese using two-pronged forks. Delicious!

GLOSSARY

aggressive, 23	Ready to fight or quarrel.
diverse, 4	Different or varied.
effigy, 18	The likeness of a person or thing.
guilds, 17	In medieval times, these were groups, or associations, of men in the same craft or trade.
hierarchies, 23	Groups of people, animals, or objects arranged in order of rank, grade, or class.
medieval, 18	Refers to the Middle Ages, the period of European history from A.D. 476 to 1450.
migration, 21	The movement of animals from one place to another, usually when the seasons change.
pagan, 11	A person who has few, if any, religious beliefs or believes in many gods.
theme, 12	A main idea, subject, or feature.
torso, 22	The body of a human being, excluding the head, arms, and legs.

INDEX

Picture credits
Oliver Bolch: 6, 12 (bottom), 13, 14 (top); Camera Press: 10 (bottom); Haga Library: 1, 3 (bottom), 8 (bottom), 9, 10 (top), 11, 12 (top), 16, 17 (top), 18 (both), 19, 21, 22 (both), 25, 27, 28; Blaine Harrington: 3 (top), 4, 14 (bottom), 15; HBL Network: 2; International Photobank: 5, 26; North Wind Picture Archives: 8 (top), 24; Photobank Photolibrary: 7 (top), 17 (bottom), 20; Topham Picturepoint: 7 (bottom), 23

Digital scanning by
Superskill Graphics Pte Ltd